C000172088

My Pen and I
With Many
Observations

Nigel Millett

THE CHOIR PRESS

First published in the United Kingdom in 2022 by
The Choir Press

ISBN 978-1-78963-275-0

My photographs ... their origins, locations & birthdate

Cover photo: of characterful old door at a tumbled down house in Crete 2012

Back cover: I have a fascination for tree bark & their patterns, Scotland 2021

Smooth lines intro: Thames barge anchored off East Head, West Sussex 2021

Amusing lines intro: a cheeky stone flower trough Charlestson house, East Sussex 2021

Wavy lines intro: a giant fir cone on a wooden open book shaped plinth, the Trossachs National park 2021

Contents

WAVY LINES Stand up & wave … someone will wave back   1

A good question   2
Betterment   3
Blow out the candles   4
Bosham Hoe   5
Golden wedding   6
Heavenly Harmonies   7
Loco about Loco's   8
Lots of 'ings   9
Resting   10
Rhythm of life   11
Seasons   12
Shadows in the Night   13
Sleepy Hollow   14
Smokey   15
Spring   16
The Chocolate Temptress   17
The great outdoors   18
This Universe   19
Truth   20
Unlocking 2021   21
Unlocking the lochs   22
Vagabond or Adventurer   23
War   24
Wine from the vine (In times gone by)   25

AMUSING LINES Smile & the world smiles with you

AMUSING LINES Smile & the world smiles with you   27

A Little Nonsense   28
A Rotter   29
A shoreside stroll   30
Alabaster   31
An Amphibian Life   32
Enough   33
Ethel   34
Meet Pete   35
Mona Lisa   36
My delusional friend   37
On the Street   38
Shamrock   39
Siblings   40
Squelch   41
The Arboretum   42
The Cheese Platter   43
The Hoarse Horse   44

SMOOTH LINES Let's not get ruffled   47

Celebration   48
Chestnuts   49
Dancing in the breeze   50
Dawning   52
Embrace   53
Flying buttresses   54
Flowing   56
Food of love   57

Food for the mood   58
Gratitude   60
Time   61
Move forward   62
My life is good   63
My shoulder   64
Never Quit   65
The Sky Tonight   66
Smiles & thanks   67
Song   68
The shape of words   69
Darkness & Light   70
Longest Night of the year   72
The dog & the tortoise   73

To my daughters
Qanita and Bianca

Foreword

Please enjoy the words I have
written,
some whilst in despair, some
whilst smitten

They are thoughts that
occasionally dropped into my
consciousness that
I would like to share ...

WAVY LINES

Stand up & wave ...
someone will wave back

A good question

What inspires you to write a poem
Says the paper to the pen
Oh I don't know I get picked up
Put to paper as & when
It is then & only then
The poem starts to form
With many notes & scribbles
Until it starts to flow
Or comes in drabs & dribbles
Sometimes ... hitting a plateau

But to answer your original question
Which I have evaded thus far
It is often inspired by something I read or hear
Sometimes something I see ...
Like a planet or a star

Maybe soon we'll be obsolete ... out on a wing
Says the pen to the paper, with ...
Computers, word processors, smartphones
And all that kind of thing
But ... I will always touch your paper
We shall see what it may one day bring

Betterment

Hope is fuel for the body
Almost as necessary as water or food
A fuel to be shared by offering kindness
Sharing is good for the mood
Kindness will offer empowerment
Something we should all learn as we grow
Having hope & kindness, not blindness
These traits should be something we sow
This all breaks down as betterment
Because giving hope costs us nothing
But is oh so worthwhile

Blow out the candles

I believe it is your Birthday
Happy Birthday to you I say
Let's hope you have a lovely time
Do all that you want today
Birthdays are not quite so exciting
As the years come and go
But they are nevertheless special
So give those candles a blow
Because it is your anniversary on files
Don't think that you are too old
Each day of every year is for fun and smiles

Bosham Hoe

Waves … *slam one another, awash in their own white saliva,
   breaking apart at the harbour entrance, energy searching
   for a beach head, a haven … for those weathered boats.*
*This harbour of Bosham … as beautiful … as a mermaids
   bosom, usually covered with soapy surf, lapping at the
   brackish earth.*
Oh … Bosham Hoe
*Where tides flow, high & low, fast not slow … can catch you
   out unless you know … these waters … can be your
   friend or your foe …*
*Flooding once a common occurrence, made many men
   quake, especially those from the insurance.*
Oh … Bosham Hoe
*There was a time when salty, sweet, tender oysters were
   found & harvested here, discarded shells from that time,
   now help form the cloisters of the church.*
*Oh … Bosham Hoe, may the tides continue to flow, to
   welcome & harbour the weary mariner to re-emerge with
   regained strength, for yet another nautical surge!*
Oh … Bosham Hoe
*As the sun shines, even when it rains, tides come … tides
   go, yet the beauty remains.*
May the winds & the tides always freshen her
*Whilst old Canute sits at the shoreside in his throne like chair,
   mourning the loss of his beautiful young daughter, sadly
   drowned in the Millstream, he now awaits a high tide to
   wash away his heavy pains.*

Golden wedding

50 years since they were wed
50 years legally sharing a bed
50 years of tears & joy
50 years in which to annoy … each other

But all these years have not been wasted
Because love & tolerance has been tested
Now during their autumn years
It will be laughter & smiles
Without any tears

Dedicated to my sister & brother-in-law 2021

Heavenly Harmonies

One evening whilst drifting through the woods
Heavenly harmonies could be heard floating in the air
What could be the source of this wondrous sound
Beyond doubt neither cicadas, wolf or a bear
Those euphoric notes appeared to be weaving
Through the trees to reach ones soul
They certainly make one feel as if one is dreaming
Maybe the sounds will consume and console
As I wonder searching in my heart, the heart that has been
*   heavy of late*
Is it just a moment, a moment in time
Or maybe it is purely my fate
However, a new dawn is over the horizon
And then the sun will arise once again
My eyes they will open and widen
See all that is before and around me
Along with the sounds of that beautiful siren
Drifting in and around the woods

Loco about Loco's

There is nothing more nostalgic than a steam train
Chugging and puffing along the line
As it clatters and rattles along those rails
Playing that old sweet song, always in time
The shunting and hissing, buffers kissing
Passengers reminiscing about journeys long ago
Journeys through valleys and mountains
Long dark tunnels where time stands still
Oh how we wished those journeys would last
Not leaving a station until ...
The guard whistles and waves his flag for all clear
Those memories still evoke a tear I fear
The smoke from the engine, smuts in the eye
This doesn't make the journey less romantic
Especially at night on the railway sleeper ... oh my
Rocking from side to side, sleep getting deeper and deeper
That marvellous old engine stuck in the sidings
Longingly looks at the sleek electric model whizzing past
There was once a day he was also considered fast
I wonder how long sleek electric will last
Before he runs out of steam
Rack and pinion, cog and narrow gauge
Railways have evolved since George Stephenson's Rocket
   was the rage
Then the Mallard and Flying Scotsman
Now it's Hideo Shima's Bullet train taking centre stage

Lots of 'ings

Buds bursting
Leaves showing
Flowers blooming
Bees buzzing
Birds singing
Cocks crowing
Farmers sowing
Gardeners mowing
Clocks changing
Daylight extending
Temperature rising
Spring springing
Winter disappearing
Hooray

Resting

I lay here on my day bed
With eyes gently closed
Do you think I may be dead?
I lay here on my day bed
I lay here …
Just resting my weary head

Rhythm of life

Leaves are falling …
They float and they dance
They twist and they turn
Through the air then to the ground
Creating a carpet so crisp
So colourful & so crunchy
They crackle as we walk around
The colour of many a hue, russets, gold and brown
I've yet to see a leaf that's blue, have you?

It's amazing that as one day
These leaves will naturally break down
Then feed the trees from whence they came
And seeds will also be sown

This happens each and every year,
Nature is truly so wonderful
So wonderful it needs not man
But man needs nature …
I fear

But if man disappeared off the face of the earth
Then nature would truly flourish
It would resemble a new birth
While this planet becomes newly nourished

Seasons

I am witnessing some early signs of Spring
Does that indicate Winter is at an ending?
It makes me feel good to realise
Spring is on its way
In front, not behind us
Yet not too far away

So let us now look forward
Keeping Winter well at bay
Making plans for the times ahead
Enjoying each & every day

Shadows in the Night

She emerges like a living ghost
Down in that shack by the track
Never ever seen in the light of day
Only the dim light of the night
By the light of passing trains
Flitting between and through shadows
I wonder ... what is her plight

Whatever her life pertains
Would she be offended if confronted
Does she need assistance or help
Or is she maybe self contained
Some folk are content left alone

Should I approach and offer provisions
Or should I leave her as she remains
Turn around and mind my own
Stop thinking about those propositions

Sleepy Hollow

I see a path I'd like to follow
Where will it lead me?
Maybe down to Sleepy Hollow

A new path for me
Is like an adventure
To meander along it
With my filly while I clench her

We will run, we will trot
We may gallop or canter
Along that winding path
To wherever it may take us

I certainly know not
Oh I do like to trot
Along with my favourite filly
Along any unknown path

Smokey

I have replaced you with cigarettes
That intoxicates as you once did
They burn away in my fingers
As our love
Yet I have no regrets

They don't leave that same sweet smell
That used to linger on my skin
But for all that I have lost
I will cherish
And learn not to dwell or sin

Spring

I hear the birds, I hear them sing
They fly up high in the air
Take to their wing

Flying high in the sky
Soaring up to the sun ...
We cannot catch them, even when we run!

They swoop and they soar
They dart and they dive
Oh how I envy those birds, what a life they do live!

They can travel so far without bus, plane or car ...
They require no money
Just enjoy life
Now ain't that funny?

The Chocolate Temptress

Chocolate from heaven
Created by an angel
Such wonderful aromas
Such delicate flavours
Chocolate melted in a pan
Hearts melt where she stands
Tempts those to come & savour
Food of the gods
Created by an angel
For meeting this Chocolatier
I shall be . . . .
Forever grateful

The great outdoors

During the summer we tend to forget
English winters can be cold, damp & wet
The ground becomes soggy
Sometimes quite boggy
Sometimes frosty, rarely snowy
But indoors can be nice & cosy

It is not a good season for camping
But camping is such a fun event
Laying under the stars looking for mars
Or sound asleep in a tent

When awakened by the golden sun
You can go & bathe in a chilly river
Then afterwards go for a run
Or stand on the riverbank & shiver

This Universe

They say there are more stars in the night sky
Than grains of sand on the land
I find this so difficult to comprehend
What about all our deserts, beaches & oceans?

Is all this due to the birth of our earth
Or is it because the universe is infinite
And this planet we live on is not
Or are there billions of martians & aliens
Shining torches that appear to us as dots

They say there are ten thousand stars
For every grain of sand on earth
Are there just so many quasars
Or am I just creating mirth

This universe is over thirteen billion years old
With one hundred billion galaxies
Our galaxy is the Milky Way I am told
An answer will one day come & it will all unfold

Truth

The shrouds of uncertainty have enclosed me
The positivity of my mind deserted me
Our lives deserve better
Our own love must not falter
If we are to be true to ourselves

To find true love and respect
We alone must love ourselves first
Otherwise ...
Our love will always thirst
Never to be quenched
Yet always drenched
Under that sodden shroud

Unlocking 2021

There's a rumour we're coming out of lockdown
Is Boris setting us free?
Will we be able to socialise
In groups of more than three?

We may even be able to travel
By air, land or sea
Oh I do so enjoy travel
It enriches my mind and me

Twelve months of lockdown it has been
But has not been too tedious thus far
Soon we'll be visiting the pub
Drinking coffee, beer or cider at the bar

Lockdown has helped many be creative
Thinking outside the box of the box
Sadly deprived us of social & physical contact
However I learned how to make fabulous socks

Unlocking the lochs

The mystery of the lochs
The majesty of the glens
The bens with their soaring heights
Secreting fantastical dens
No longer presided over by feuding clans
Instead overseen by majestic eagles

Lochs reflecting the light of the sky
Beside shadows of the colossal bens
Majesterial in all its beauty
It all makes me feel I'd like to fly
Soaring & sailing from these waters & up
Up high alongside that acrobatic eagle

Such views must be had from being so high
Higher even than that far distant steeple
Almost touching the clouds in this azure blue sky
Far away from the crowds & the busy people

The beauty & bounty of these wonderful shores
Should not be underestimated.. it is a larder of lots
Elusive otters & beavers creating more dams, mini lochs
Oh those great deceivers

Fish in abundance, salmon, eel & trout
Ospreys & eagles they have a good rout
Feeding on this plentiful abundance
Here or thereabouts …

Vagabond or Adventurer

The life of a vagabond is a free life
A vagabond is not always down and out
Sometimes it is simply a choice
A choice to be free, no encumberance you see
Without any chains, shackles or nagging voice
Is it a life many would like to tackle
Wandering freely from place to place
To sleep on a bench under a leafy tree, no shackle
You'll never know where he may be
It could be in the park, sometimes with dogs that bark
If approached too suddenly

Often he appears clean
Sometimes dirty, sometimes scruffy, sometimes shabby
Often seen late at night
Whilst sleeping by a headstone near the abbey
So if a vagabond life you may like to lead
Even if only for a month or so
Think carefully before you ...
Cut loose, pack a few things and just let it go

War

So glad am I not to have had to fight in a war of any kind
To me, war is just not right …
To me, war is a total blight!

If there are winners … who are they?
Certainly not the ones having to fight!
Maybe it's the arms and chemical manufacturers,
Landowners, shareholders and ones on the far right

War with arms never solves any problems or disputes
It just cheapens the lives of the men and women who make
    up the troops
Diligently following orders from their superiors at the rear …
Clearing the way to make the path safe and clear

Not only are precious lives lost, also beauty in the form of our
    world
Beautiful bridges, buildings, history, mountains, nature, land
    and sea
Why did we destroy these? Can someone please explain
What is it all about? Please, please, please tell me.

The war may eventually finish, but the scars they still remain
Not only on the land, but also on the brain
Who for? And what for?
What is the gain?
Can someone please, please explain

I have been fortunate, unlike so many …

Wine from the vine
(In times gone by)

Walking along the many rows of vines
Handpicking grapes to be made into wine
For savouring & relishing ... enjoying
Whilst they dined

To create ...
They picked, removed stems then crushed
Next pressed ... in a large vat with their feet
This gave quite a rush, as it all gradually
 turned to mush, but took great care
 not to crush ... the bitter seeds

The juice then strained, poured into containers
Left for many weeks for natural gases to escape
The skins of the grape creating yeast for fermentation
But held back a while, not yet ready for drinking

Fermentation began as the yeast mixed with sugars
This combination then produced CO_2 & alcohol
Which after much patience became heavenly, delicious wine
Oh my, oh my, how truly divine ...

(A footnote (ha ha) apparently yeast is also found between toes
So this may have been another source for the fermentation)

AMUSING LINES

Smile & the world smiles with you

A Little Nonsense

The sea that you see
Begins with an ' S ' not a 'C'
And you had better believe me
Because if you look you will see
That it is so, in the dictionary
You see ...

****

Oh out there on the briny
Where the sea appears so shiny
On a calm & sunny day
Yachts becalmed without wind
Tacking to port & starboard
Being outraced by a wayward turtle
Scuttling along without sail or fin
No worries as it is well armoured
Above & below waves it does hurtle
Oh that amusing wayward turtle.
Maybe he'll be first to the harbour

A Rotter

Andy Trotter, you are a rotter
For making us feel so bad
We did not mean to offend you
Now I feel quite sad
It was all 'Last of the Summer Wine' banter
Not directed purposely at you
The words that we used
Were meant as good fun
Please do not feel abused

A shoreside stroll

I hear waves crashing on the rocks
I see a soapy wash of breaking waves
The seaweed smells of dirty socks
Crabs exposed turn about and scuttle
Mussels clinging with all their might ...
On rocks while limpets hold on
Putting up a superhuman fight
As if held with super holding glue
Maybe that soapy wash is residue
From the bathing mermaids earlier shampoo
Should the crabs shampoo the seaweed
So that it no longer smells like dirty socks
And hang it out to dry on those boulder like craggy rocks

Alabaster

Alabaster, Alabaster is white all right
Alabaster, Alabaster it shows in the night
To find Alabaster you don't need a light
Because Alabaster is white all right
It can sometimes be other colours
Varying from yellow to brown, or duller
But that is normally due to where it is found in the ground
Or simply just uncovered
By you …

An Amphibian Life

I am a frog on a lily pad
Basking in the sun
I cannot stay here too long
Or I may get burned on my bum

The lily pad is like my day bed
After spending so long in the cold, damp mud
It is somewhere warm to rest my head
As I get so stiff now that I am an old crud

We frogs drink water through our skin
So we don't sunbathe for too long
Otherwise we get far too dry, unable to grin
Also any predator may come along

A frogs predators can be birds, lizard or snake
On the lily pad I can spy them ...
Hopefully before a meal of me they make
If any attack on me is attempted ... I can plop into the water
Where I feel safer, more protected and hide ... before it's full
*   scale slaughter*

The lily pad is also my table
A good spot for catching my lunch
Those heavenly insects so yummy
I need quite a lot to fill my tummy

Croak ... Ribbit ... Croak

Enough

She says, I've had enough!
Enough of what I say
You really wouldn't understand
I need to get away
To go …
Where are you going
May I lend a hand …
To pack your bags, your clothes & things
And send you to a far off land
Where the palm trees sway

Ethel

I heard two ladies talking
Whilst in the park today
One said her name was Ethel
The other, Ethel May

Now Ethel
May or may not have known
That the other lady, Ethel May
Is on her way to some place
Very, very far away

But Ethel, not wanting to appear nosey
Or enquire as to where Ethel May heads
So she just carries on talking
Whilst walking around the rose beds

Now Ethel May is becoming agitated
Knowing she has a train to catch
Not wanting to give too much away
Says I really must leave this patch

Meet Pete

Four men on the golf course
With eight balls between them
My god! You really should have seen them
Swings to the left
Balls to the right
One almost hit a lady
Gave her such a fright
Whilst going to apologise
And retrieve his round, white ball
The lady said to Pete
A man like you I was hoping to meet
And here you are
With your balls at my feet

Mona Lisa

A lady such as this
I did not know could exist
But here she is, like the Mona Lisa

She has that same serene smile
But oh, how she does rile
Especially when I try to tease her
To be teased she enjoys
And gives as good as she takes
Yet she is so full of magic, doesn't realise, that's tragic

There is a hole in her belly
But we all have those
Though hers is not smelly ...
It smells like a rose
That leads me to those two other holes
And they are right at the end of her nose

Let's not look for bad, only for good
If we see that in all
It will be like eating a good pud!

My delusional friend

I have a good friend named Alan
Who is under delusion you see
Because he thinks I am his brother
This causes terrible confusion you see
As the folks we both know, know my mother
And my mother begat not he

It all began some time back
Someone mistook him for me in the sea
Well I must tell you
I was quite upset at the time
He is far more rotund than me

Of course, Alan being Alan
Encouraged this mistaken identity
And so, after many years to date
I'm afraid I'm stuck with this similarity

Maybe it is my fate ...

On the Street

The people you meet
Whilst walking the street
One never knows who one may greet
It may be Mrs Jones in her favourite seat
Sitting on that bench in the shade from the heat
She always smiles and is very sweet
Or Mrs Higginbotham can be rather dour
Her smile I'm afraid is rather sour

Shamrock

She's a 1966 baby
Born on St Patrick's Anniversary
Nudging St Patrick to the side that day
She said move over please for me
I would like to share your special day
Yes ... there is room said he
Then giving her a freshly picked shamrock
Asking how many leaves do you see?
She answers, I would like to see four
But in fact I see only three

Siblings

They say we were brother and sister, we two
In former lives
Do you think that could be true?
She the brother, and I the sister
I suppose it could be so
Some may say that is cuckoo
And I don't look good in a dress
Do you?

When I study her face I see so much more
It is just like opening a very secret door
A doorway into her inner being
And I find it really hard to believe what it is I am seeing ...
Such beauty

Those beautifully shaped eyes
They reveal a beauty so wise
What a privilege to experience
I have a beauty too ...
But to find it
You must look inside my shoe

What a pair we are if this is true
Let what we have, be preserved
But please, no, no, not in a jar or a shoe!

Squelch

Trudge, trudge through the sludge
Through the mud we go
Why is it often so mucky
After the dazzling white snow?

Snow, initially so pretty
When melting becomes quite slushy
No wonder I end up sliding around
On my bottom … now very mucky

Melting ice creates similar conditions
Or many days of downpours
It dampens the ground
Now best to walk very carefully
If you do not want to be found
Laying on your bottom
Involuntarily!

The Arboretum

The willow weeps
The Scots pine
The chestnut towers
Creating wonderful bowers
The elder isn't old
The oak stands majestic
The elm stands bold
While the larch forms an arch
The maple offers syrup
The pear is not just two
The plane doesn't fly
But a plum or two will do
As it makes a decent pie
The walnut is so healthy
The sycamore stands so big
Its rotating blades spinning to the ground
For the squirrels to bury and birds to dig
Let us not forget the graceful willow
With long dangling tendrils all around
Trailing down and down and down
To that luscious fertile ground

The Cheese Platter

It was on the platter that they met
In conversation said Brie to Stilton
"What is it that makes you sweat
Your aroma overwhelms me
Because in that state you become so smelly
So please move over ... you are ...
Tainting my fragrant bouquet"
Not good in the deli

When I am in that state, I become quite soft and gooey
Really tasty, not too chewy
I soften like butter in your hand
And the aroma I give off is rather grand
I'm often enjoyed with a pleasant Bordeaux claret
But I won't go on and on like a parrot

Why are your veins so blue, are you cold?
Or is it because you are aging and old?
But you too are also delicious I am told
What about you, friendly Cheddar?
You look so luscious and strong
Is that because you matured in the gorge
And you don't have too strong a pong

Cheddar said ...
"If you get together with Stilton
I think you could create a lovely aroma
And in the months to come
You may have lots of Gorgonzola"

The Hoarse Horse

My voice is hoarse
You will of course
Understand this I'm sure
I'll do all that I can
In the most natural way I can
To find myself a cure

I don't mind a hoarse voice
As long as I don't start to neigh
So I will try hard to find the cure
To keep that neigh at bay
If then I begin to grow a tail
I will then not neigh, but wail!

SMOOTH LINES

Let's not get ruffled

Celebration

Today there is a Birthday
For someone I'm sure somewhere
Birthdays are not just for someone
But for many anywhere

To celebrate these occasions
Calls for special celebrations
Yet not all may feel this way
But who knows what it may bring

For some it may be sadness
For others love and joy
But sadness will hopefully be overcome
And be replaced with gladness
Not leaving one feeling numb or glum

Gladness is a wonderful state
But things sometimes get in the way
Do not let sadness, only gladness
Invade your special day

Try to be happy come what may …

Chestnuts

It is a January day
The sky is so grey
The cloud hangs low
And the time goes slow
I awaken in the dark
In a few hours, again will be dark
So I sit beside the fire
Roast chestnuts from my perch
Listening to the choir
Sing in the neighbouring church

Dancing in the breeze

As I lay on this mossy carpet of green under the sunlit trees
Gazing upwards as the leaves float & dance softly in the
    breeze
A nearby rabbit jumps up to sneeze, blowing leaves as they
    fall
Disturbing the crows all sat in a row, silencing their noisy row

Wind now building undressing the oaks
Removing their russet leaf rustling cloaks
Creating another carpet on the ground below
A carpet of golden brown twisting leaves

These trees they then appear to shiver
Or do they merely in the breeze quiver
Oaks standing so fast with their roots so deep
Stretching & searching for an underground river

As the breeze gathers tempo & the temperature drops
Breeze now a wind building to a crescendo
With those leaves now swirling
No longer floating & dancing

Chestnut cases split & open everywhere
By those squirrels for their winter larder
Burying with the acorns
Before the climate changes & becomes too
much harsher

The sun becoming now lower in the sky
Temperatures dropping as days go by
Migratory birds gathering on the wires
Before their journey south to a brighter sky

Dawning

A mountain range rises out of the distant haze
Such a view as this never fails to amaze
The rising of the clouds
Those pinnacles released from the shrouds
Creating such wonderful displays
The shafts of sunlight and the green of the trees
Ochres, greens and grey reflected onto the rocks
Flocks of swirling, gliding birds soar above the trees
When the sun is at its zenith the view is ablaze
Oh my, I could watch this splendour for days and days
Until the sunlight dips the last of its golden rays
And we then await a fresh new dawn

Embrace

Your voice makes me quiver
Those lips
They deliver
A passion unrivalled before

Our lives, they have merged
Our passion has surged
To a level not experienced before

I embrace you today
And I hope that I may
Embrace you for many more!

Flying buttresses

That magnificent old church at the top of the hill
Built as a monument by folk of iron will
The beautifully crafted stonework
Such craftsmanship ... gives me a thrill
Worked from crudely self drawn plans
Sketched with only parchment & quill

Those masons of ages back in the past
Couldn't have foreseen how long this monument
would last ...
Men with great foresight, vision & strength
Determination, adoration, great art & skill
Certainly knew how to build & went to great length
With only crude tools to fulfill ...
Not with the machinery as used today

Its spire is so staggeringly high ...
Built with timber & stone ... certainly no steel
The very sight of that spire truly makes my head reel
It soars so high up to the sky
Appearing to have written its own history
Up there amongst the fluffy white clouds
Creating much mystery
Pointing straight up to the stars
The sun, the moon & mars
A haven for bats & birds of prey
While congregations kneel inside to pray

The pillars, buttresses & the strength of angels
Help lost souls find their way
Amid the gargoyles, pinnacles & vaults
Vestibules, vestries, arches at great angles
Galleries, transepts, chancels & bell tower
What a tribute to those men with great skills & great power

This church has stood five hundred years
Surviving wars, battles & tempest
Many skilled men, women & children lost
Tears shed, tears shared all at quite a cost
All for this magnificent, wondrous conquest

Flowing

A meandering stream
A wandering dream
Flows in & around my mind
Where will this dream lead me
I hope it will be gentle & kind

Flowing through heath & meadows
Fields & orchards green
Where will this meandering stream take me
As it ebbs & flows in my dream
I hope it just flows & flows
While nothing intervenes

Food of Love

I thought it was just a passing in our lives
Not expecting to fall into a bed of chives
Chives add beautiful flavour to food
Good food, it nourishes & lightens the mood
Just as love nourishes the soul
Not feeling like a goldfish
In a goldfish bowl
Chives & fish, what a wonderful dish

Food for the mood

I have a passion for music
Music I do like to play
Listening to music most days
Never ever fails to amaze

It can be any style or genre
Swinging from opera to jazz razzamatazz
Each stirring me in differing ways
Often leaving me in a blissful daze

Opera usually stirs different emotions
Compared to jazz, blues or rock
Then there is of course classical
This should never, ever be mocked

Music evolved from the sounds of nature
Wind rustling through bushes & trees
The knocking together of branches
And the whisper of the breeze

The many calls from the birds
The humming of the bees
These sounds contribute to the music
I certainly hope this music is never disturbed

Instruments were created replicating these sounds
Then when all brought cleverly together
Orchestras hold no bounds
Those sounds can become extremely profound

Whatever genre or style playing
I'm sure often brings a smile or tear
Even a reverberating singing bowl
Music is good food for the soul & the ear

Gratitude

Gratitude is a state of grace
Sadly expressed by too few
Graciousness experienced by even fewer
Are so many people so incomplete?
By just offering a few words of gratitude
Life could be so sweet
Gratitude and graciousness costs so very little
Yet, is oh so very rewarding
Can people not see how much better a world they could live in
All they need to offer is gratitude
A little – no, a lot
Of graciousness
Can you imagine all those happy, smiling faces?
People happy having received gratitude for whatever they
    may have done
Gratitude to the multitude
No wars
Just love
To everyone
Thank you
    Thank you
        Thank you

Time

When did time accelerate
So quickly
It was only yesterday I was a grandchild
But today I now find myself
A Grandpape …
Yet still my mother's child

This rapid passing of time
Makes one realise
To live each and every day
Live those days fully and truly
In every possible way

We must not let time pass us by
Like a car whizzing along the lane
In a hurry …
Savour each moment
Enjoy the surroundings
Your family, friends and …
Do not hurry or worry

Move forward

From love to loved is where we are now
Oh why has this happened?
Oh why or how?

So many good times
So much has been shared
Not just physical
Not just mental
Our hearts fully bared

From the depths of despair
To a life in repair
I've now served my purpose
So …
Move forward and be happy
Live life
And take care

My life is good

My life is good
I have my health
I now have the pleasure of manifesting my wealth
This wealth I will use
In the best ways that I can
To create joy and prosperity
And help those who cannot
I shall try to enlighten them and help make their lives more full
But I will not charge in to do so, like a fool or a bull

To see people smile makes these things so worthwhile
What does it cost …
A little time, maybe lots
A little patience and tenderness and all is not lost

My shoulder

I was there for her ... yes, at the right time
She needed a shoulder
It happened to be mine
A strength, a joke, kind words and understanding
This helped keep her stable and stopped her meandering

Never Quit

No matter what ... when at a low ebb
There is always hope ...
Always something not on the web
Maybe better than where you find yourself
Not to be found in a book on the bookshelf

The solution is often in your head
Determination will help you find
Believing that things will get better
A better place, better state of mind

Looking the problem in the eye
Whilst peering at the mirror
Seeing your true beauty
And then start to apply ...
Those positive strategies
That were hidden away
Buried deep somewhere

Hope can help us spring into action
To see things once again more clearly
Hope encourages satisfaction with more clarity
Looking out at the world before reaction
Go on try it ... this is not merely theory
Nor is it merely reaction

The Sky Tonight

We have a full moon tonight
But the sky is overcast
I'd like to see the moon so full
How long will this cloud last?

To see the moon fills me with joy
This has always been my thing
It has been affecting me a while now
Since I was a wee young boy

The moon affects so many things
Its energy is so strong
From oceans, plants and everything
Without it the world would go all wrong

So let us all appreciate
This wondrous silver ball
It lets us know the time of day
While owls peel off their call
T'wit t'wit t'woo!

Smiles & thanks

A smile goes a mile
A scowl is just fowl
What does it cost?
A smile is never lost

A word of thanks
Can break through ranks
Combine thanks with a smile
And the world is yours

Give thanks, thanks, thanks

Song

I have a song I like to sing
I like it more than anything
Singing all day from when I awake
Oh I do love that song
I will never forsake

To sing with joy lifts the spirit so high
Music & lyrics resonating through the soul
Oh my … how I enjoy singing that song
Even when I am out of control
Having sung several notes totally wrong

Lyrics & music so personal & evocative
Can make one cry, whilst singing happily
Echoing … filling one with joy
I find them oh so totally provocative
Stirring fond memories or even sad

A song is never ever bad!

The shape of words

The shape of those eyes
The turn of her face
Oh I cannot believe how it made my heart race

The words that she spoke
So wise and so sound
It made my head reel
Around and around

But steadying myself
And standing fast
I did not realise
That this love would last …
But it does!

Darkness & Light

At this time of year there is so much darkness
How wonderful it is to create some light
Creating light by lighting a candle
Everyone enjoys seeing a light at night
Even when it is not very bright

Light offers hope from any angle
Hope to someone lost in the dark
Hope to the mariners on a wild stormy sea
Hope with the dawning of a bright new day
Hope & memories for you or for me

Festivals have grown to celebrate the light
Because light gives life ...
All around the globe folk create fantastical sights
With lights floating up in the dark starry skies
Lights afloat on the dark flowing waters

From Buddhism to Judaism
Catholicism to Hinduism ... also Sikhism
All of the people love a bright shining light
Reminding them of stars & moon at night
Making a prayer or a wish for their sons or daughters
In their town or village or special quarter

From Grandchildren to Grandparents who do not falter
Festivals of light bring a sparkle or even a tear to the eye
A spectacle to be recalled as the years pass by
A candle can always be lit in any place of worship
One can create ones own altar ... give thanks , pay homage
... feel exalted!!

Longest Night of the year

During the longest darkest night
We need a light
To light our way forward
To help ease our plight

These long winter nights
Are a natural occurrence
When the earths axis
Tilts away from the sun

In the northern hemisphere
This is an annual occurrence
Whilst the southern hemisphere
Has its longest day & you can run
Run for longer ... having fun in the sun

But in the south they don't escape
The shorter days & longer nights
It is a continual eternal cycle
A never ending inscape ...
Another wonder of this amazing planets delights

The dog & the tortoise

Dodi the dog out exploring one day
Tumbled across Tonto the tortoise
Sluggishly walking out in the woods
Dodi said hello good morning to you …
Do you fancy a race can you match my fast pace
It is time to come out of your shell & show your face

Tonto stayed in his shell & flipped himself over
Started rolling away over that lovely soft clover
Gathering a pace going faster & faster
Leaving Dodi the dog standing
All wide eyed, bewildered, shaking & ranting
Thinking I'll show that tortoise who can be fastest

Rolling quickly Tonto was gaining a lead
While running fast Dodi was gathering speed
Both racing downhill now with Tortoise ahead
There's a stream … at the bottom Dodi gets
Filled with dread.
Which is a good thing for Tonto
Because he can't lessen his speed

So Dodi being a smart dog lay down on all fours
Along the bank of the stream with head on both paws
He then awoke in his basket to find it was all
Just a dream … come on Dodi let's go do the chores
Calls a voice …

Lightning Source UK Ltd.
Milton Keynes UK
UKHW020841070322
399675UK00006B/21